GARDEN COOKBOOK

Rob Rees

Published 2009 by
A & C Black Publishers Ltd.
36 Soho Square, London, W1D 3QY
www.acblack.com

ISBN HB 978-1-4081-0860-4
PB 978-1-4081-1299-1

Series consultant: Gill Matthews

This book is produced using paper that is made from wood grown in managed, sustainable
forests. It is natural, renewable and recyclable. The logging and manufacturing processes
conform to the environmental regulations of the country of origin.

Produced for A & C Black by Calcium.
Printed and bound in China by C&C Offset Printing Co.

All the internet addresses given in this book were correct at the time
of going to press. The author and publishers regret any inconvenience
caused if addresses have changed or sites have ceased to exist, but
can accept no responsibility for any such changes.

Acknowledgements
The publishers would like to thank the following for their kind permission
to reproduce their photographs:
Cover: Dreamstime: Ireneusz Sinicki; Shutterstock. **Pages:** Dreamstime:
Claudio Baldini 4b, 20tr, Susabell 15; Istockphoto: Piotr Antonów 18tr, 19,
Toby Creamer 13b (main), Floortje 7, Marek Pawluczuk 6tl, Peter Seager 6tr;
Shutterstock: Titov Andriy 14tl, Andrjuss 10tl, Norman Chan 16tl, Elli 9, S.
Fierros 10tr, Douglas Freer 14tr, Magdalena Kucova 8tr, Robyn Mackenzie 17,
Monkey Business Images 11, 21, Newo 20tl, Ostromec 12tr, Marek Pawluczuk
16tr, Vishal Shah 4t, 8tl, Rui Vale de Sousa 18tl, Bartosz Wardzinski 13b
(inset), Dusan Zidar 12tl. **Illustration:** Istockphoto: Ronnie Sampson.

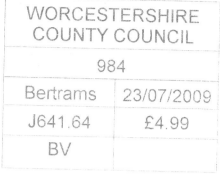

Contents

Food is Fun

Cooking and growing food can be a lot of fun. Sharing a meal with friends and family is also a great way to spend time together. Inside this book you'll find lots of fun recipes to make tasty dishes.

Cooking with the seasons

You can see different fruits and vegetables in the garden at different times of the year. We call these divisions in the year the "seasons".

The recipes in this book use some of the fruits or vegetables from each of the four seasons: spring, summer, autumn, and winter. Simply follow the instructions on each page...

Beetroot can be grown in the autumn.

Peas can be grown in the summer.

Some recipes need more attention or more time to make.

How to use your ingredients.

Tips straight from the chef.

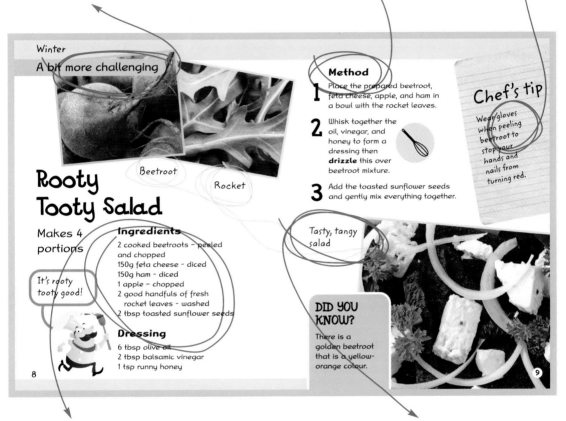

Winter

A bit more challenging

Beetroot

Rocket

Rooty Tooty Salad

Makes 4 portions

It's rooty tooty good!

Ingredients
2 cooked beetroots – peeled and chopped
150g feta cheese – diced
150g ham – diced
1 apple – chopped
2 good handfuls of fresh rocket leaves – washed
2 tbsp toasted sunflower seeds

Dressing
6 tbsp olive oil
2 tbsp balsamic vinegar
1 tsp runny honey

8

Method

1 Place the prepared beetroot, feta cheese, apple, and ham in a bowl with the rocket leaves.

2 Whisk together the oil, vinegar, and honey to form a dressing then **drizzle** this over beetroot mixture.

3 Add the toasted sunflower seeds and gently mix everything together.

Chef's tip
Wear gloves when peeling beetroot to stop your hands and nails from turning red.

Tasty, tangy salad

DID YOU KNOW?
There is a golden beetroot that is a yellow-orange colour.

9

Everything you will need to make the recipe.

The finished product!

REMEMBER!

Always ask an adult before using the kitchen to make these recipes.

Leeks   Potatoes

Leek and Potato Soup

Makes 4 portions

Ingredients

2 large leeks –
washed and sliced
25g butter
2 medium potatoes – peeled,
washed, and diced
600ml vegetable stock
250ml semi-skimmed milk
Freshly ground black pepper
Grated nutmeg

Serve with crusty bread.

Method

1 Fry the leeks gently in the butter for 3 minutes. Stir frequently.

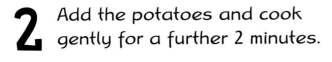

2 Add the potatoes and cook gently for a further 2 minutes.

3 Add the milk and stock and bring to the boil.

4 Reduce the heat and **simmer** until the potatoes are cooked (about 25 minutes).

5 Blend in a liquidiser or with a hand blender.

6 **Season** with pepper and grated nutmeg.

Ta, da! Delicious soup

Chef's tip

Chop off the **frayed** green ends of your leeks. They are too **bitter** to eat.

DID YOU KNOW?

Leeks are packed full of vitamins to help fight colds.

A bit more challenging

Beetroot

Rocket

Rooty Tooty Salad

Makes 4 portions

It's rooty tooty good!

Ingredients

2 cooked beetroots – peeled and chopped
150g feta cheese - diced
150g ham - diced
1 apple – chopped
2 good handfuls of fresh rocket leaves - washed
2 tbsp toasted sunflower seeds

Dressing

6 tbsp olive oil
2 tbsp balsamic vinegar
1 tsp runny honey

Method

1 Place the prepared beetroot, feta cheese, apple, and ham in a bowl with the rocket leaves.

2 Whisk together the oil, vinegar, and honey to form a dressing then **drizzle** this over beetroot mixture.

3 Add the toasted sunflower seeds and gently mix everything together.

Tasty, tangy salad

DID YOU KNOW?

There is a golden beetroot that is a yellow-orange colour.

A bit more challenging

Ginger

Rhubarb

Crunchy Sweet 'n' Sour Bake

Makes 4 portions

Ingredients

500g rhubarb
50ml water
100g caster sugar
200g plain flour
100g butter
125g demerara sugar
1tsp ground ginger

Serve with custard or ice cream.

Method

1 Preheat oven to 200°C/gas mark 6.

2 Wash the rhubarb then cut diagonally.

3 Place in a saucepan with the water and caster sugar. Cook gently until the rhubarb begins to soften.

4 Place the mixture in an **ovenproof** dish.

5 Put the remaining ingredients in a bowl. Rub between your fingers to make crumbs.

6 Sprinkle the crumbs over the rhubarb to cover it.

7 Place in the oven for 20 minutes until golden and crisp.

Mouthwatering rhubarb and ice cream

DID YOU KNOW?

Pulling rhubarb out of the ground keeps it fresher than cutting it.

Asparagus

Avocado

Asparagus and Guacamole Dip

Makes 4 portions

Ingredients

1 bunch of asparagus - washed

4 handfuls of mixed salad
   leaves, to garnish

2 ripe avocados

4 fresh tomatoes

Juice of half a lemon

1 tsp ground black pepper

Get dipping!

Method
To make the dip

1 Cut each avocado in half lengthways. Carefully remove the stone.

2 Scoop out the insides into a bowl. Mash into a smooth paste with a fork.

3 Mix in the lemon juice and pepper.

4 Dice the tomatoes roughly and stir them into the creamy mixture.

To cook the asparagus

1 Remove the bottom 2 cm from the asparagus.

2 Cook the asparagus in boiling water for 2 minutes.

3 Drain the asparagus through a **sieve**.

4 Serve warm or cold.

Yummy asparagus and guacamole dip

DID YOU KNOW?

Asparagus is a **relative** of the lily flower.

13

Fruit Smoothie

Raspberries

Bananas

Makes 4 portions

Ingredients

125g fresh strawberries
125g fresh raspberries
1 ripe banana, sliced
250g natural low-fat yoghurt
300ml semi-skimmed milk
6 to 8 ice cubes

Experiment with other fruits and flavoured yoghurts.

Method

1 Wash the berries.

2 Place fruit, yoghurt, and milk into a blender or food processor and **purée** until smooth. Add a little extra milk if you want it to be thinner.

3 Add the ice cubes and blend again for a further 20 to 30 seconds until the ice is roughly crushed. Serve immediately.

Really fruity fruit smoothie

Chef's tip

Raspberries can quickly **spoil**. It is best to keep them in the fridge until you are ready to use them. Wash them just before using.

DID YOU KNOW?

Fruit smoothies are packed with the **vitamins** that keep your body in tip-top shape.

Strawberries

Lemon

Strawberry Zinger

Makes 4 portions

Ingredients

1 **punnet** of strawberries
1 lemon
4 slices of sushi ginger
(available from most supermarkets)
2 level tsp icing sugar

Serve in a bowl with clotted cream and shortbread biscuits.

Method

1 Wash strawberries and remove the green tops.

2 Cut strawberries into four pieces and put in a bowl.

3 Finely chop and add the ginger.

4 Grate half the lemon zest and add to the bowl.

5 Squeeze the juice from the lemon and add to the bowl.

6 Sieve the icing sugar into the bowl.

7 Mix the strawberries around a couple of times – be gentle though!

8 Leave them for 10 minutes before serving.

Sugary sweet strawberries

DID YOU KNOW?

27,000 strawberries and 7,000 litres of cream were eaten at the Wimbledon Tennis Championships in 2007.

A bit more challenging

Pears

Mint

Sticky Toffee Pears

Makes 4 portions

Ingredients

4 pears – washed
50g butter
100g demerara sugar
200ml whipping cream
Sprig of mint – roughly chopped

Pears are also delicious in salads with **vinaigrette.**

Method

1 Cut the pears into four pieces and remove the core.

2 Melt the butter in a frying pan.

3 Add the pears and cook gently until golden.

4 Stir in the sugar gently, whilst turning the fruit.

5 When the sugar starts to melt add the cream.

6 Bring to the boil and keep boiling until the cream is thick.

7 Remove from heat and add the chopped mint. Serve with a scoop of vanilla ice cream.

Scrumptious pears and ice cream

DID YOU KNOW?

In 1640 there were only 60 types of pear. Today there are over 3,500 types.

Easy

Mint

Peas

Mushy Peas

Makes 4
portions

Ingredients

200g fresh peas taken from the pod
50g mashed potato (still warm)
25g butter
1 tbsp chopped fresh mint
Pinch cracked black pepper
Some milk (if needed)

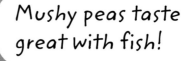

Mushy peas taste
great with fish!

Method

1 Place the peas in a saucepan and just cover with boiling water. Cook the peas for 2 minutes.

2 Drain the liquid away through a sieve. Add the mashed potato to the peas.

3 Stir in the butter and mush everything together. Add a drop of milk if it looks a bit dry.

4 Stir in the mint and cracked black pepper just before serving.

Minty and mushy peas

DID YOU KNOW?

The world record for eating peas with chopsticks is 7,175 peas in 1 hour.

Glossary

bitter when something tastes very sharp and not sweet

drizzle to cover very lightly

frayed ragged and torn

grated shredded, using a metal grater

ovenproof dish that can be placed in a hot oven

punnet a container that holds fruit

purée to mash or blend until smooth

relative belonging to the same family group

season to improve the flavour by adding herbs or spices

sieve a container with holes. When a mixture is placed inside a sieve, the liquid is drained from it, but the solid material is left behind

simmer to cook on a very low heat

spoil to go off or start to rot

vinaigrette salad dressing made from oil, vinegar, and seasoning

vitamins the goodness in food that keeps bodies healthy

Further Information

Websites

Find out how different foods are grown at different times of the year and how to cook with them at:
www.eattheseasons.co.uk

Discover how to eat healthily at:
www.eatwell.gov.uk

Find out which foods your body needs to work properly at:
www.nutrition.org.uk

Learn how you can help the environment by reducing your food waste at:
www.lovefoodhatewaste.com

Books

Children's First Cookbook: Have Fun in the Kitchen! by Annabel Karmel. Penguin Books (2005).

Cooking up a Storm by Sam Stern. Walker Books (2005).

Star Cooks – Recipes by Celebrity Chefs. Dorling Kindersley (2006).

Index